Spotter's Guide to
BUTTERFLIES

George E. Hyde
Illustrated by Joyce Bee

Contents

Editorial Director
Sue Jacquemier

Editors
Su Swallow, Sue Tarsky

Designer
Sally Burrough

Additional illustrations by
Christine Howes

Printed in Great Britain

First published in 1978 by Usborne Publishing Limited, 20 Garrick Street, London WC2

Reprinted 1985

Text and Artwork © 1978 by Usborne Publishing Limited

How to Use this Book

This book is an identification guide to some of the butterflies of Britain and Europe. Take it with you when you go out spotting.

The butterflies are arranged in order of the families to which they belong. Each one is shown both with its wings open and with its wings closed, because the wing markings on the underside are often quite different from those on the upperside. Most butterflies rest with their wings closed in the evening and on dull days, and feed with their wings open in the daytime.

The butterflies in the book are shown on one of the plants they like to visit for a drink. Sometimes the caterpillar is also shown with the plant it eats. If male and female butterflies of the same kind vary in size and markings, both male and female are shown to help you to identify them. (The symbol ♂ means male and ♀ means female.)

The description next to each picture tells you about the butterfly – special markings, where it lives, or which flowers it likes to visit. It also

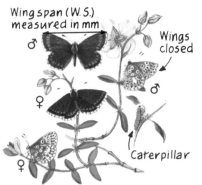

Wing span (W.S.) measured in mm

♂

Wings closed

♀

♂

Caterpillar

♀

gives the average wing span (shortened to W.S.), measured across the widest point. The butterflies in the book are all drawn life size, except where the text tells you otherwise.

You may find the information on page 49 and the glossary on page 60 useful when you are reading the descriptions.

Scorecard

Next to each description is a small blank circle. When you spot a butterfly, make a tick in the circle. The scorecard at the end of the book gives you a score for each butterfly you spot. A common butterfly scores 5 points, and a very rare one 25 points. You can add up your score after a day out spotting.

Areas Covered by this Book

The yellow area on the map shows the countries covered by this book, although not all the butterflies that live in these countries are included. Some butterflies in the book do not live in Britain, or are very rare here, but are common in other European countries. In these cases, the description will tell you that it is "not in Britain," or the countries where it *is* found.

Watching Butterflies

If you want to catch butterflies to study them closely, you will find a net useful. You could make one like this yourself, or buy one.

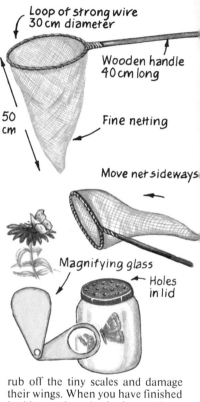

Loop of strong wire 30 cm diameter

Wooden handle 40 cm long

50 cm

Fine netting

Move net sideways

Magnifying glass

Holes in lid

To catch a butterfly in a net, approach it quietly and don't let your shadow fall on it. Watch where it settles and bring the net over it gently, with the opening sideways on. Then flick the bottom of the net up over the metal loop to stop the butterfly from escaping.

When you have a butterfly in the net, place the open end of a glass jar over the mouth of the net and slip the lid on. Use a magnifying glass to look at the antennae and the tiny scales on the wings.

Keep a detailed record of the butterflies you find. To identify them, look at the markings on both sides of the wings and the shape of the wings. It will help to identify the plant the butterfly was resting on.

Look for butterflies in spring and summer. A good time to see them is in the evening, when many of them rest on grasses.

If you catch butterflies, remember that they are extremely fragile. Handle them very carefully and don't touch their wings. If you do, you will rub off the tiny scales and damage their wings. When you have finished looking at them in the jar, set them free.

Butterfly or Moth?

You can spot the difference by looking at these points.

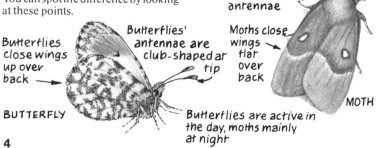

Butterflies close wings up over back

Butterflies' antennae are club-shaped at tip

BUTTERFLY

Hardly any moths have club-shaped antennae

Moths close wings flat over back

MOTH

Butterflies are active in the day, moths mainly at night

Monarch

Also called Milkweed. Rare
visitor from America and the
largest butterfly found in Britain.
Visits bramble, ragwort and
other flowers.
Open places.
W.S. 103-106 mm.

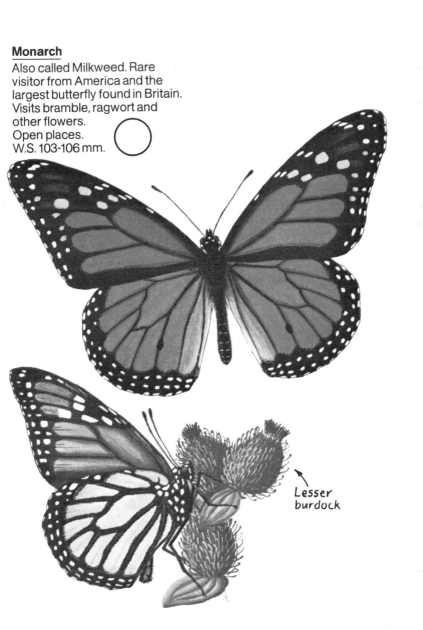

Lesser
burdock

5

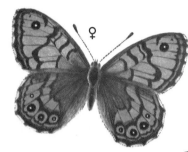

Wall Brown

Often rests on walls and
paths. Likes rough, open
ground and woodland
glades. Flies slowly.
Caterpillar eats
grasses.
W.S. 44-46 mm.

Caterpillar

Large Wall Brown

Often settles on stony
paths in hills and
mountains.
Not in Britain.
W.S. 50-56 mm.

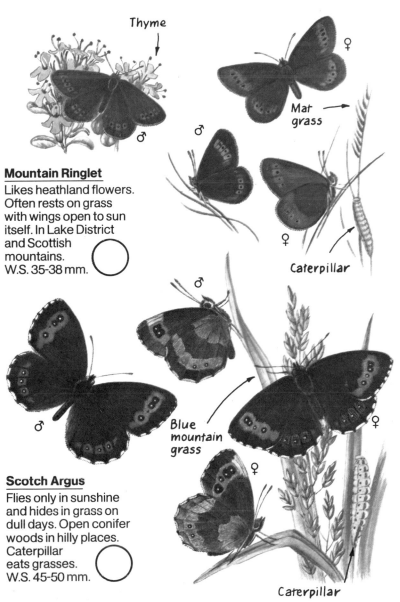

Thyme

♀

Mat
grass

♂

♂

♀

Caterpillar

Mountain Ringlet

Likes heathland flowers.
Often rests on grass
with wings open to sun
itself. In Lake District
and Scottish
mountains.
W.S. 35-38 mm.

♂

♀

Blue
mountain
grass

♀

Scotch Argus

Flies only in sunshine
and hides in grass on
dull days. Open conifer
woods in hilly places.
Caterpillar
eats grasses.
W.S. 45-50 mm.

Caterpillar

Orange-brown European form ♂

♀

Bramble

Speckled Wood

Likes bramble flowers.
Often settles on
sun-spotted leaves in
woods and forests.
Caterpillar
eats grasses.
W.S. 47-50 mm.

♂

♀

Arran Brown

May visit flowers but rests
mostly on grasses. Open
grassland, near woods or
forests. Not
in Britain.
W.S. 48-54 mm.

Grayling

May visit field scabious
and other flowers, but
mostly rests on the
ground with wings closed.
Sandy places and
chalk downs.
W.S. 56-61 mm.

Great Banded Grayling

Likes lucerne and other
flowers, but mostly rests
on the ground with
closed wings. Open
woodland.
Not in Britain.
W.S. 66-72 mm.

Lucerne

Knapweed

Marbled White

Flies in meadows and grassy fields. Likes thistles, knapweed and other roadside flowers. Caterpillar eats grasses. W.S. 53-58 mm.

Large Ringlet

Rests mainly on grasses. In mountains. Caterpillar eats grasses. Not in Britain. W.S. 42-46 mm.

Meadow Brown ▶
Meadows and grassy places where it visits thistles, knapweed and bramble flowers. Active even on dull days. Caterpillar eats grasses.
W.S. 50-55 mm.

Bramble

◀ Ringlet
Keeps to damp, grassy places and sunny woodland paths. Visits thistles, knapweed and bramble flowers.
W.S. 48-52 mm.

Thistle

Hawkweed

◀ Small Heath
Not fussy about where it lives, and found in open woods, on marshes and on dry hillsides.
Likes hawkweed.
W.S. 33-35 mm.

♂

♀

♀

♂

Gatekeeper
or Hedge Brown

Basks in sunshine on roadside hedges, especially on bramble. Most common in the south. W.S. 40-46 mm.

Bramble

The colours of this butterfly vary a lot

♀

♂

Heather

♀

♂

Large Heath

Sometimes visits heath flowers, but mostly rests on grasses with wings closed. Likes damp places. Caterpillar eats moorland grasses. W.S. 33-35 mm.

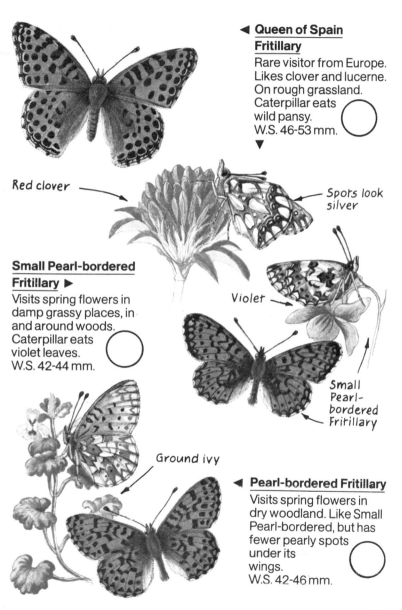

◄ Queen of Spain Fritillary

Rare visitor from Europe. Likes clover and lucerne. On rough grassland. Caterpillar eats wild pansy. W.S. 46-53 mm.

Red clover

Spots look silver

Small Pearl-bordered Fritillary ►

Visits spring flowers in damp grassy places, in and around woods. Caterpillar eats violet leaves. W.S. 42-44 mm.

Violet

Small Pearl-bordered Fritillary

Ground ivy

◄ Pearl-bordered Fritillary

Visits spring flowers in dry woodland. Like Small Pearl-bordered, but has fewer pearly spots under its wings. W.S. 42-46 mm.

The butterflies on this page
are smaller than life size

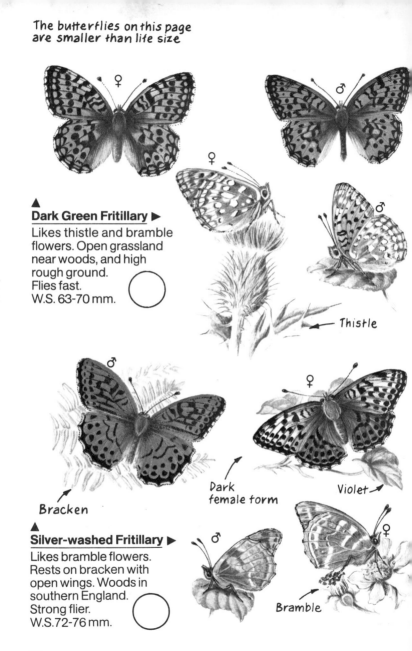

Dark Green Fritillary ▶

Likes thistle and bramble
flowers. Open grassland
near woods, and high
rough ground.
Flies fast.
W.S. 63-70 mm.

Thistle

Bracken

Dark
female form

Violet

Silver-washed Fritillary ▶

Likes bramble flowers.
Rests on bracken with
open wings. Woods in
southern England.
Strong flier.
W.S. 72-76 mm.

Bramble

14

◀ Violet Fritillary

Visits spring flowers in light woodland, on heaths and in meadows. Often in hilly places. Not in Britain.
W.S. 32-34 mm.

Niobe Fritillary ▶

Likes thistles. In grassy places on mountains, but only up as high as trees grow. Not in Britain.
W.S. 48-60 mm.

Violet

These butterflies are smaller than life size

◀ Cardinal Fritillary

Likes thistles and lime tree flowers. Look for it in flowery meadows. Caterpillar eats leaves of violets.
Not in Britain.
W.S. 72-80 mm.

Thistle

Heath Fritillary ▶

Only found in woodland where cow-wheat grows. May also visit plantain flowers. Southern Britain, but rare. Caterpillars are eaten by pheasants. W.S. 40-44 mm.

Caterpillar

Cow-wheat

Devil's bit scabious

◀ Marsh Fritillary

Visits spring flowers in marshy places. Lives in colonies (or groups). Notice shiny wings. Caterpillar eats devil's bit scabious and honeysuckle. W.S. 42-48 mm.

Plantain

Caterpillar

Glanville Fritillary ▶

Rough grassy slopes by the sea. Only found on the south coast of the Isle of Wight. Caterpillar feeds on plantains. W.S. 41-45 mm.

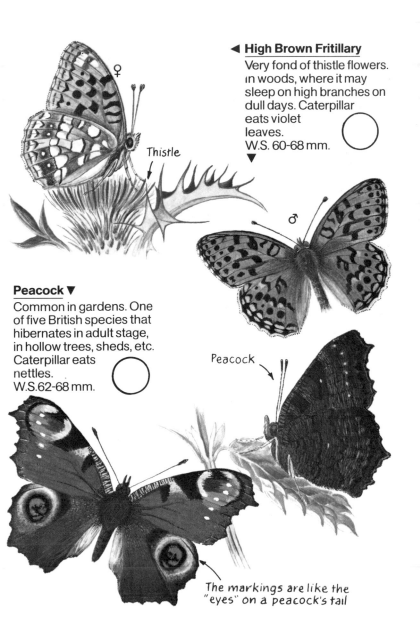

◄ High Brown Fritillary

Very fond of thistle flowers. In woods, where it may sleep on high branches on dull days. Caterpillar eats violet leaves.
W.S. 60-68 mm.
▼

♀

Thistle

♂

Peacock ▼

Common in gardens. One of five British species that hibernates in adult stage, in hollow trees, sheds, etc. Caterpillar eats nettles.
W.S.62-68 mm.

Peacock

The markings are like the "eyes" on a peacock's tail

◀ Painted Lady

Arrives in spring from North Africa. Lays eggs on thistles. Adult insects can be seen in autumn, but do not survive the winter.
W.S. 62-65 mm.

Red Admiral

Painted Lady

Red Admiral ▶

Common in gardens on buddleia and Michaelmas daisies. Migrates here from North Africa. Caterpillar feeds on nettles.
W.S. 66-68 mm.

Thistle

Small Tortoiseshell

◀ Small Tortoiseshell

Name comes from pattern on wings. Visits many flowers and is common all over Britain. On the wing from April to November.
W.S. 48-52 mm.

Large Tortoiseshell ►·
Rare. Likes bramble
flowers. Rests on leaves
of tall trees in lanes
and edges of woods.
Caterpillars feed on elm
and goat
willow.
W.S. 62-66 mm.
▼

Camberwell
Beauty

◄ Camberwell Beauty
Rare visitor from
Scandinavia, and does not
breed in Britain. Yellow
wing borders turn white
with age. On hills and
visits
gardens.
W.S.70-73 mm.

Cranberry Fritillary

In bogs and swampy places. Lays eggs on cranberry, which the caterpillar feeds on. Not in Britain. W.S. 34-42 mm.

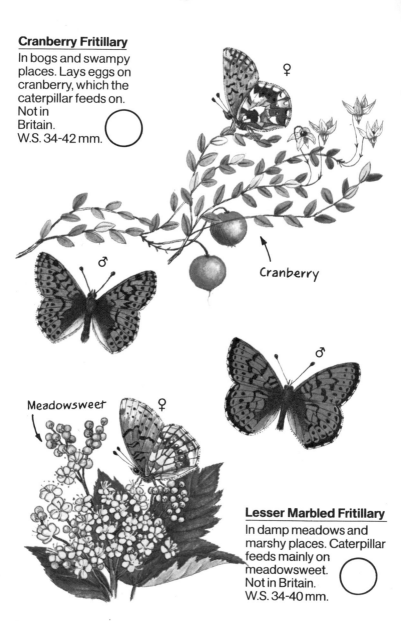

♀

♂

Cranberry

Meadowsweet

♀

♂

Lesser Marbled Fritillary

In damp meadows and marshy places. Caterpillar feeds mainly on meadowsweet. Not in Britain. W.S. 34-40 mm.

Comma

Easy to recognize by its ragged wing edges and the shape of a letter "c" on underside of its wings. In woods and gardens.
W.S. 56-58 mm.

Comma ♂

Comma

♀

Comma

Willow

Smaller than life size

When Lesser Purple Emperor's wings catch the light they shimmer purple

Lesser Purple Emperor

Does not visit flowers, but drinks from puddles and may settle on dead animals. In woods. Lays eggs on poplar and willow.
Not in Britain.
W.S. 66-70 mm.

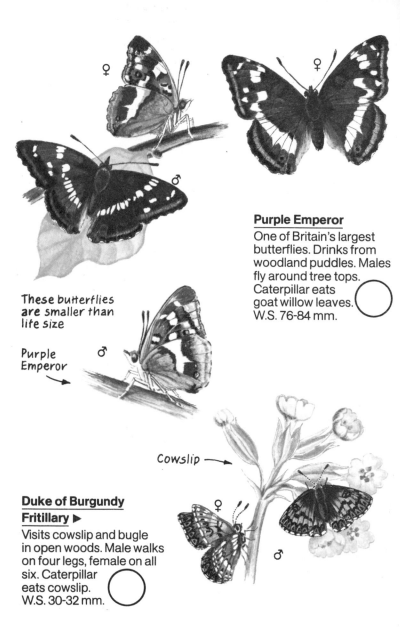

♀

♀

♂

Purple Emperor

One of Britain's largest
butterflies. Drinks from
woodland puddles. Males
fly around tree tops.
Caterpillar eats
goat willow leaves.
W.S. 76-84 mm.

These butterflies
are smaller than
life size

Purple
Emperor

♂

Cowslip

♀

♂

Duke of Burgundy
Fritillary ▶

Visits cowslip and bugle
in open woods. Male walks
on four legs, female on all
six. Caterpillar
eats cowslip.
W.S. 30-32 mm.

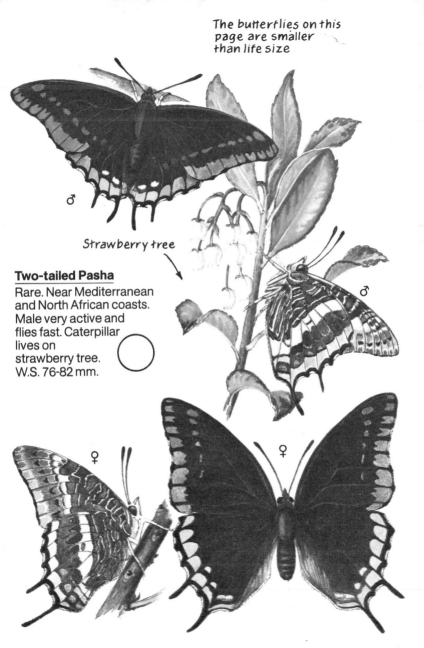

The butterflies on this page are smaller than life size

Strawberry tree

Two-tailed Pasha

Rare. Near Mediterranean and North African coasts. Male very active and flies fast. Caterpillar lives on strawberry tree. W.S. 76-82 mm.

♂

♂

♀

♀

Small Blue ▶

Britain's smallest butterfly.
Adult and caterpillar both
seen on kidney vetch.
Found in groups on
downs and
rough grass.
W.S. 20-28 mm.

Kidney
vetch

♀

♂

♀

◀ Idas Blue

Visits trefoils and other
flowers on mountain
slopes. Caterpillar eats
trefoil, and later lives
in ants' nests.
Not in Britain.
W.S. 28-32 mm.

♂

Bird's foot
trefoil

♂

Cranberry

Cranberry Blue ▶

Butterfly and caterpillar
both feed on cranberry,
which grows on moorland
and mountain slopes.
Not in
Britain.
W.S. 26-28 mm.

♂

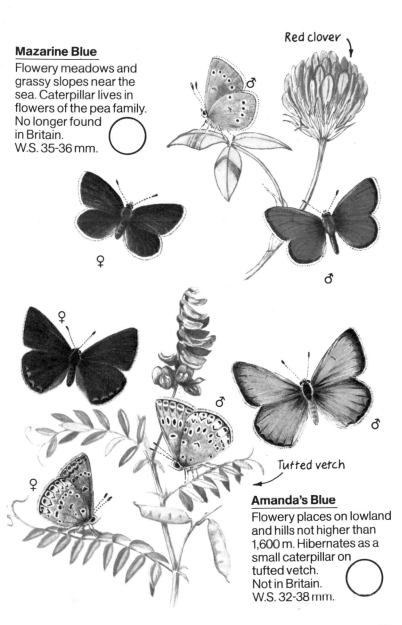

Mazarine Blue

Flowery meadows and grassy slopes near the sea. Caterpillar lives in flowers of the pea family. No longer found in Britain.
W.S. 35-36 mm.

Red clover

♂

♀

♂

♀

♂

♂

Tufted vetch

♀

Amanda's Blue

Flowery places on lowland and hills not higher than 1,600 m. Hibernates as a small caterpillar on tufted vetch. Not in Britain.
W.S. 32-38 mm.

Brown Argus

Usually flies on chalk
downs and limestone hills
where rock rose grows.
Visits flowers on warm
sunny days.
Flies fast.
W.S. 28-30 mm.

♂

♂

♀

Common
rock rose

♀

Caterpillar

Hoary
rock rose

The markings of this
butterfly vary —
sometimes it has
no white spots

Mountain or Scotch
Brown Argus

Easily recognized by the
white dot on front wing.
Sheltered moorland and
grassy roadsides in
Scotland. Visits
rock rose.
W.S. 28-30 mm.

Bird's foot trefoil

The female sometimes has more blue or less blue on her wings

♀

Caterpillar

♀

♂

Common Blue
Size and markings vary. Found almost everywhere, but prefers downs and rough meadows. Caterpillar eats bird's foot trefoil.
W.S. 28-36 mm.

♂

Horseshoe vetch

Adonis Blue
The male is our brightest blue butterfly. Two broods, in spring and summer. Chalk downs. Caterpillar eats horseshoe vetch.
W.S. 30-36 mm.

♀

♀

♂

♂

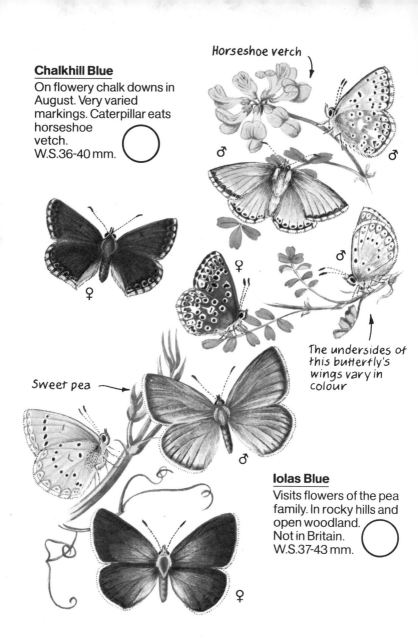

Chalkhill Blue

On flowery chalk downs in August. Very varied markings. Caterpillar eats horseshoe vetch.
W.S.36-40 mm.

Horseshoe vetch

♂

♂

♀

♂

♀

The undersides of this butterfly's wings vary in colour

Sweet pea

♂

Iolas Blue

Visits flowers of the pea family. In rocky hills and open woodland. Not in Britain.
W.S.37-43 mm.

♀

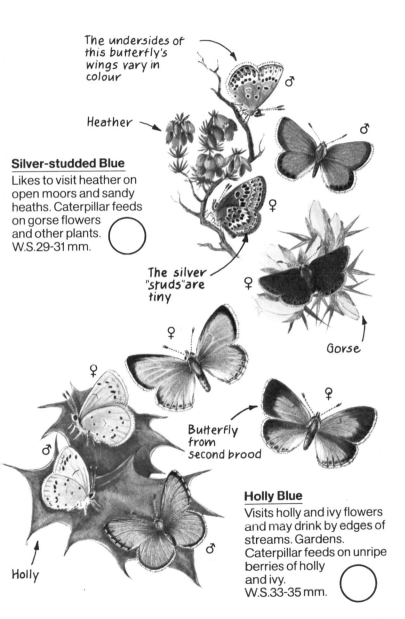

The undersides of this butterfly's wings vary in colour

Heather

Silver-studded Blue

Likes to visit heather on open moors and sandy heaths. Caterpillar feeds on gorse flowers and other plants. W.S.29-31 mm.

The silver "studs" are tiny

Gorse

Butterfly from second brood

Holly Blue

Visits holly and ivy flowers and may drink by edges of streams. Gardens. Caterpillar feeds on unripe berries of holly and ivy. W.S.33-35 mm.

Holly

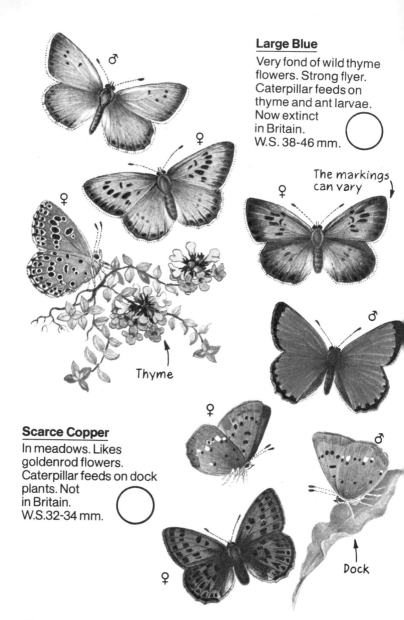

Large Blue

Very fond of wild thyme flowers. Strong flyer. Caterpillar feeds on thyme and ant larvae. Now extinct in Britain. W.S. 38-46 mm.

♂

♀

♀

♀ The markings can vary

Thyme

♂

Scarce Copper

In meadows. Likes goldenrod flowers. Caterpillar feeds on dock plants. Not in Britain. W.S. 32-34 mm.

♀

♂

♀

Dock

Purple-edged Copper

Lives in marshy places on lowland and hills up to 1,600 m. Caterpillar feeds on docks and bistort. Not in Britain. W.S. 32-38 mm.

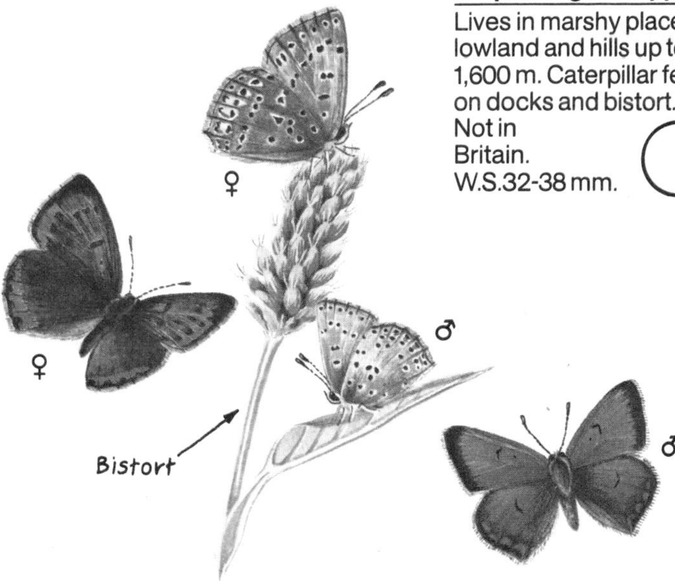

♀

♀

♂

Bistort

♂

♂

♀

Caterpillar

Small Copper

Easy to find all over Britain, especially on fleabane flowers. Female often larger than male. Caterpillar eats sorrel and dock. W.S. 26-30 mm.

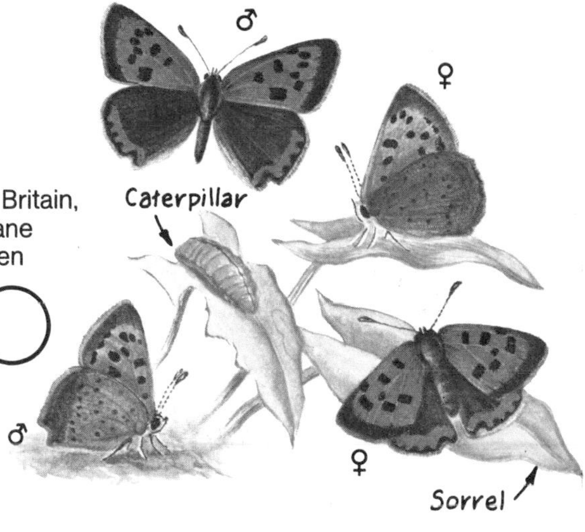

♂

♀

Sorrel

Green Hairstreak

Hard to spot because of green underwings which camouflage it on leaves. Quite common on downs, moors, edges of woods, where gorse and broom grow. W.S.31-34mm.

♂

Gorse

♂

♀

♀

Brown Hairstreak

Shy butterfly, not often seen flying. Rests on leaves of blackthorn in August and September. Edges of woods and hedges. W.S.40-42 mm.

♀

♂

♂

Notice the tails

Blackthorn

♀

Oak →

Purple Hairstreak

Flies round tree tops in big oak woods. Rests on oak leaves and visits bramble flowers. Caterpillar eats oak leaves. W.S. 36-39 mm.

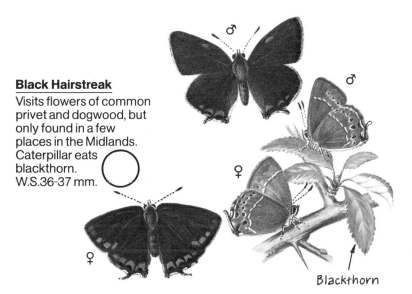

Black Hairstreak

Visits flowers of common privet and dogwood, but only found in a few places in the Midlands. Caterpillar eats blackthorn. W.S. 36-37 mm.

Blackthorn

White Letter Hairstreak

Named after white mark, like a letter "w", on underside of hind wings. Often rests on leaves of wych elm. Open woods and lanes. W.S. 34-35 mm.

Wych elm

♀

Notice the "W

♂

♀

♂

Blue-spot Hairstreak

Likes rough, hilly places with bushes. Visits privet and other flowers. Caterpillar eats blackthorn. Not in Britain. W.S. 29-33 mm.

♀

♂

♂

♀

The butterflies on this page are smaller than life size

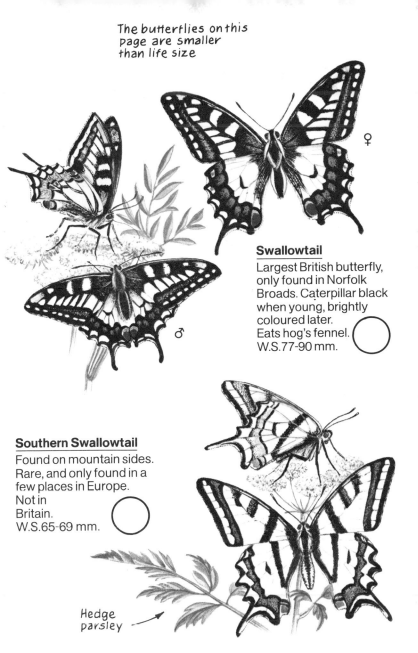

♀

♂

Swallowtail
Largest British butterfly, only found in Norfolk Broads. Caterpillar black when young, brightly coloured later. Eats hog's fennel. W.S.77-90 mm.

Southern Swallowtail
Found on mountain sides. Rare, and only found in a few places in Europe. Not in Britain. W.S.65-69 mm.

Hedge parsley

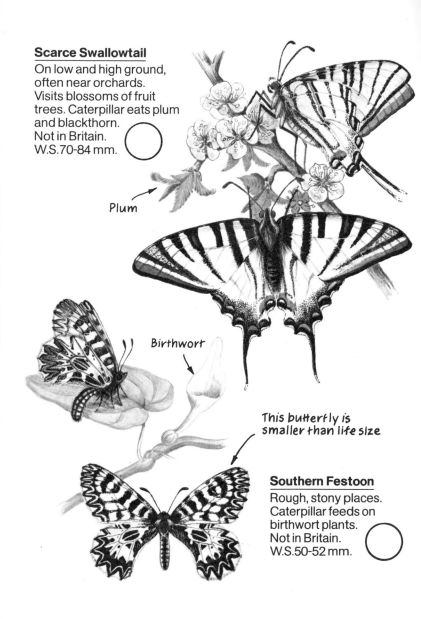

Scarce Swallowtail

On low and high ground,
often near orchards.
Visits blossoms of fruit
trees. Caterpillar eats plum
and blackthorn.
Not in Britain.
W.S.70-84 mm.

Plum

Birthwort

This butterfly is
smaller than life size

Southern Festoon

Rough, stony places.
Caterpillar feeds on
birthwort plants.
Not in Britain.
W.S.50-52 mm.

Apollo

Lives in mountains. Visits
alpine plants, especially
stonecrop flowers.
Not in Britain.
W.S. 79-84 mm.

Orpine

Small Apollo

High up in mountains,
often near streams or
damp grassland. Visits
alpine flowers.
Not in Britain.
W.S. 62-66 mm.

Reflexed
stonecrop

The butterflies on this page are smaller than life size

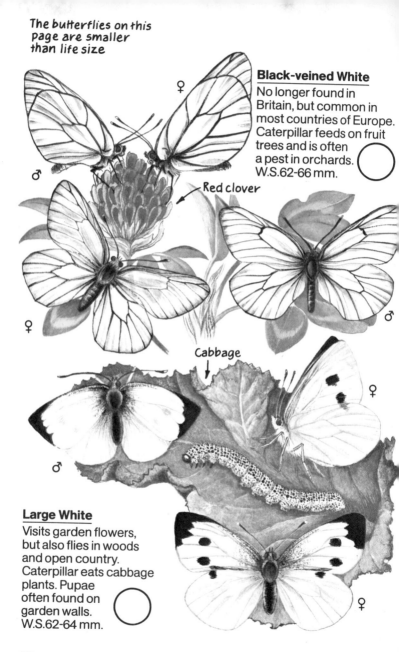

Black-veined White

No longer found in Britain, but common in most countries of Europe. Caterpillar feeds on fruit trees and is often a pest in orchards. W.S. 62-66 mm.

Red clover

♂

♀

♀

♂

Cabbage

♀

♂

Large White

Visits garden flowers, but also flies in woods and open country. Caterpillar eats cabbage plants. Pupae often found on garden walls. W.S. 62-64 mm.

♀

Small White

Appears in May and August. Lays single eggs on cabbages and nasturtiums. Common in gardens. W.S. 48-50 mm.

♂

♀

♂

♀

♂

♀

Green-veined White

Pattern on underwing helps to protect the butterfly from enemies when it sits on grass. Caterpillar eats leaves and seed pods of Jack-by-the-Hedge. W.S. 47-50 mm.

♀

♂

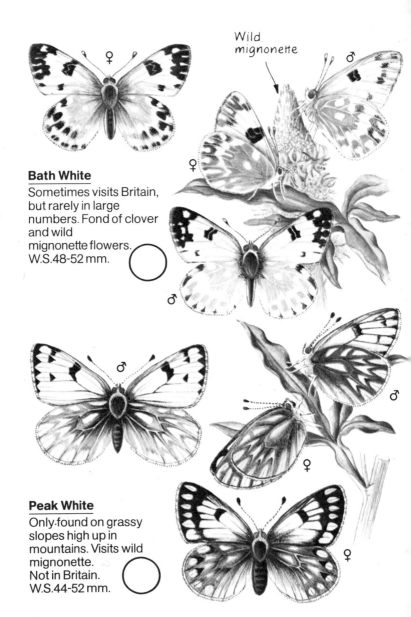

Wild mignonette

Bath White

Sometimes visits Britain, but rarely in large numbers. Fond of clover and wild mignonette flowers. W.S. 48-52 mm.

Peak White

Only found on grassy slopes high up in mountains. Visits wild mignonette. Not in Britain. W.S. 44-52 mm.

Orange Tip

Common in spring, often near cow parsley along hedgerows and edges of woods. Caterpillar eats seed pods of lady's smock. W.S.42-48 mm.

Lady's smock

Yellow vetchling

Wood White

Lives in woods, often in shady parts. Likes yellow vetchling and other woodland flowers. Weak flight. W.S.40-42 mm.

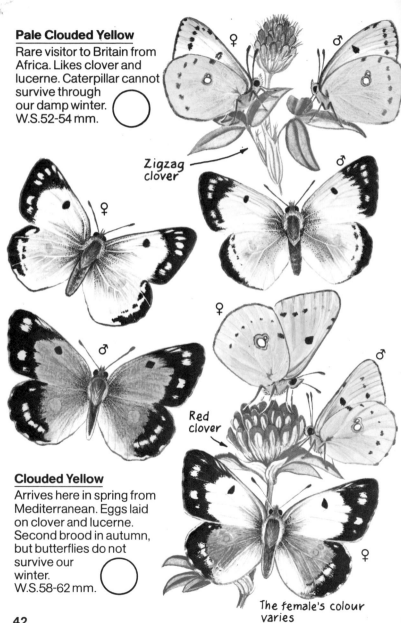

Pale Clouded Yellow

Rare visitor to Britain from Africa. Likes clover and lucerne. Caterpillar cannot survive through our damp winter. W.S. 52-54 mm.

♀

♂

Zigzag clover

♂

♀

♂

Red clover

Clouded Yellow

Arrives here in spring from Mediterranean. Eggs laid on clover and lucerne. Second brood in autumn, but butterflies do not survive our winter. W.S. 58-62 mm.

♀

The female's colour varies

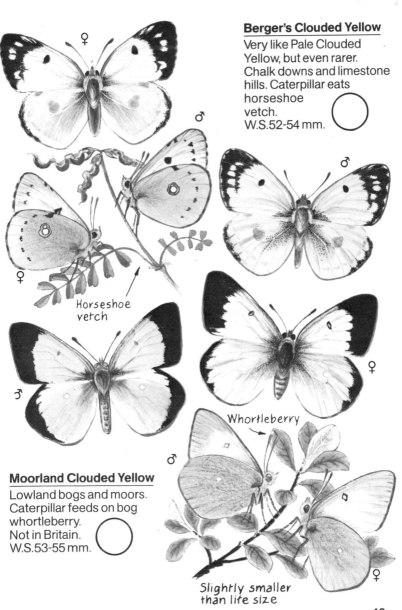

Berger's Clouded Yellow

Very like Pale Clouded Yellow, but even rarer. Chalk downs and limestone hills. Caterpillar eats horseshoe vetch.
W.S. 52-54 mm.

♀

♂

♂

Horseshoe vetch

♀

♂

♀

Whortleberry

Moorland Clouded Yellow

Lowland bogs and moors. Caterpillar feeds on bog whortleberry.
Not in Britain.
W.S. 53-55 mm.

♂

♀

Slightly smaller than life size

The butterflies on this page are slightly smaller than life size

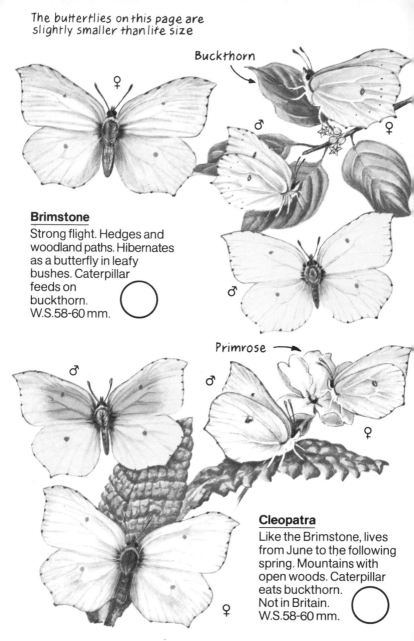

Buckthorn

♀

♂

♀

Brimstone

Strong flight. Hedges and
woodland paths. Hibernates
as a butterfly in leafy
bushes. Caterpillar
feeds on
buckthorn.
W.S. 58-60 mm.

♂

Primrose →

♂

♂

♀

Cleopatra

Like the Brimstone, lives
from June to the following
spring. Mountains with
open woods. Caterpillar
eats buckthorn.
Not in Britain.
W.S. 58-60 mm.

♀

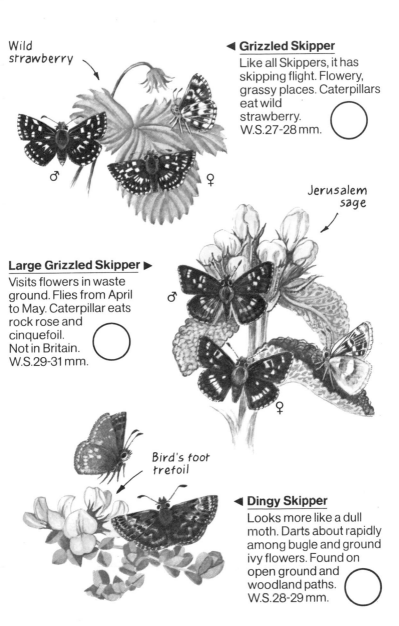

Wild
strawberry

◄ Grizzled Skipper
Like all Skippers, it has
skipping flight. Flowery,
grassy places. Caterpillars
eat wild
strawberry.
W.S.27-28 mm.

♂   ♀

Jerusalem
sage

Large Grizzled Skipper ►
Visits flowers in waste
ground. Flies from April
to May. Caterpillar eats
rock rose and
cinquefoil.
Not in Britain.
W.S.29-31 mm.

♂

♀

Bird's foot
trefoil

◄ Dingy Skipper
Looks more like a dull
moth. Darts about rapidly
among bugle and ground
ivy flowers. Found on
open ground and
woodland paths.
W.S.28-29 mm.

45

Chequered Skipper ▶

Brighter than other Skippers. Likes bugle, and suns itself on grasses in woods. Caterpillar eats brome grass.
Rare.
W.S.27-29 mm.

Bugle

♀

♂

Bugle

◀ Northern Chequered Skipper

Visits bugle and other spring flowers in woods and grassland. Caterpillar eats grasses.
Not in Britain.
W.S.27-29 mm.

♂

Large Chequered Skipper ▶

Likes damp meadows full of flowers, and shady paths in woods. Often rests on grasses.
Not in Britain.
W.S.32-36 mm.

♀

Wood false-brome

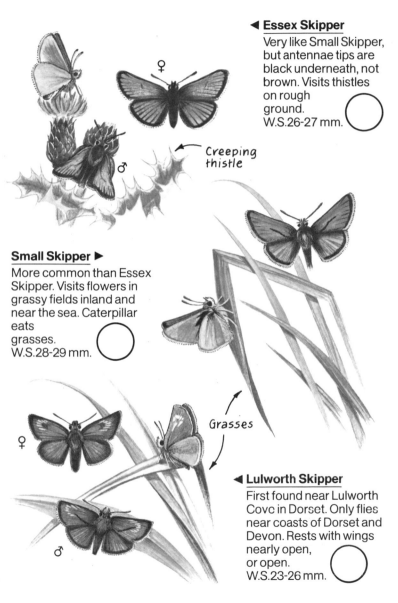

◄ Essex Skipper

Very like Small Skipper, but antennae tips are black underneath, not brown. Visits thistles on rough ground. W.S.26-27 mm.

♀

♂

Creeping thistle

Small Skipper ►

More common than Essex Skipper. Visits flowers in grassy fields inland and near the sea. Caterpillar eats grasses. W.S.28-29 mm.

Grasses

♀

◄ Lulworth Skipper

First found near Lulworth Cove in Dorset. Only flies near coasts of Dorset and Devon. Rests with wings nearly open, or open. W.S.23-26 mm.

♂

Large Skipper

Commonest Skipper.
Visits bramble and thistle
flowers in grassy lanes
and open woodland.
Flies from June
to August.
W.S.30-32 mm.

Stalkless thistle

Silver spots
on underside

Silver-spotted Skipper

Looks like Large Skipper,
but has silvery spots on
underside of hind wings.
Only found on chalk
downs. Often
rests on grasses.
W.S.31-33 mm.

Sheep's
fescue-grass

From Egg to Butterfly

Typical egg shapes

1

Butterflies lay their eggs singly, in twos or threes, or in one large cluster. Most lay them straight on to the food plant which the caterpillars will feed on. The eggs usually hatch in a few days or weeks.

2

When the caterpillar, or larva, hatches, it feeds on its food plant. Most eat the leaves. The caterpillar sheds its skin several times as it grows. Many butterflies hibernate in the larval stage.

3

When the caterpillar is fully grown, it stops eating and changes into a chrysalis, or pupa. Most pupae are fixed to plant stems by a sticky thread, either upright or hanging down.

4

The adult butterfly develops inside the pupa. When it is ready to emerge, it breaks out of the pupal skin and rests for an hour or two while its wings expand and harden.

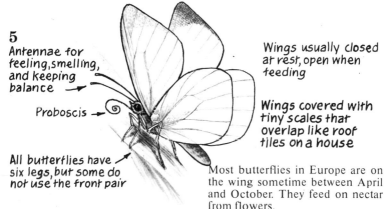

5

Antennae for feeling, smelling, and keeping balance →

Proboscis →

All butterflies have six legs, but some do not use the front pair

Wings usually closed at rest, open when feeding

Wings covered with tiny scales that overlap like roof tiles on a house

Most butterflies in Europe are on the wing sometime between April and October. They feed on nectar from flowers.

Make a Butterfly Garden

If you have a garden, you could grow flowers that attract butterflies. Butterflies visit flowers to feed on nectar, a sweet liquid which they suck up with their long tube-like tongue (called a proboscis). Some of the flowers that butterflies like are shown in this picture.

Try to plant a mixture of spring and summer flowers, to encourage a variety of butterflies to visit your garden. Make a record of which butterflies you see each month, how many of each species there are, and which flowers they visit. You can draw them too. You will soon notice which are the favourite flowers of each kind of butterfly, but a few flowers, like buddleia,

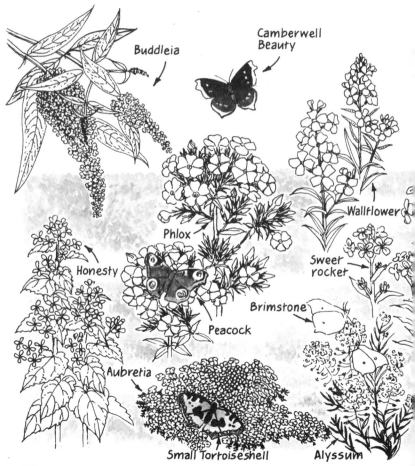

Buddleia

Camberwell Beauty

Phlox

Wallflower

Honesty

Sweet rocket

Brimstone

Peacock

Aubretia

Small Tortoiseshell

Alyssum

phlox and Michaelmas daisies, attract many different species so they are good plants for your garden.

Some butterflies like to feed on wild flowers, and many rest on grasses, so if there is room you could allow these to grow, or collect seeds in the countryside to plant at home.

A patch of stinging nettles might encourage butterflies like the Small Tortoiseshell, the Peacock and the Red Admiral to lay their eggs there. When the caterpillars hatch, they feed on the nettles.

Do not use poison sprays on your flowers because these can kill butterflies.

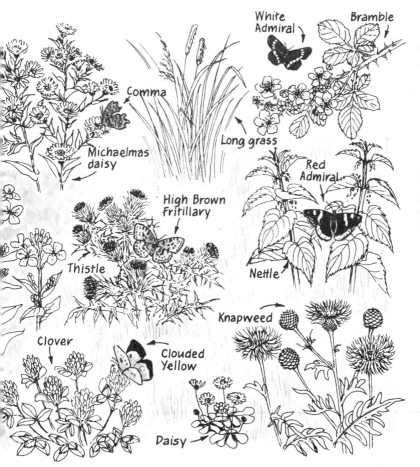

Comma

Michaelmas daisy

White Admiral

Bramble

Long grass

High Brown Fritillary

Red Admiral

Thistle

Nettle

Knapweed

Clover

Clouded Yellow

Daisy

Keeping Butterflies

Collecting Eggs

Look for butterfly eggs from about April to August. Look on leaves, stems and grasses, and remember to wear gloves to touch stinging nettles. Handle the eggs gently, and put them in a jar like the one below on a bit of the plant on which you found them. Keep the jar somewhere cool. Look at the eggs every day. When they are nearly ready to hatch they will turn from pale yellow to grey. When the tiny caterpillars hatch, they will eat part of the egg shell for their first meal but after an hour or two they will move away from the shell and will need fresh leaves from their food plant to feed on. At this point you should replace the lid with a muslin cover.

Baby Caterpillars

If you start your collection with baby caterpillars, rather than eggs, you should cut off the piece of plant you find them on and put it gently into a jar or plastic box with a muslin cover.

The baby caterpillars need fresh leaves from their food plant every day. Leave the old leaves in the jar until the caterpillars have moved on to the new ones. Do not try to move the caterpillars yourself.

Most caterpillars change their skin (called moulting) about four times as they grow. After the first moult, you should move the caterpillars to a larger jar, like the one on the opposite page.

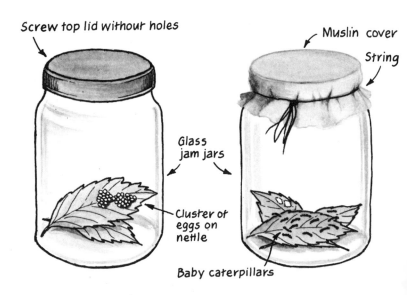

Screw top lid without holes

Muslin cover

String

Glass jam jars

Cluster of eggs on nettle

Baby caterpillars

Older Caterpillars

As soon as the caterpillars have grown a little, transfer them carefully to a larger jar like this one, which you can prepare yourself. Remove them from the glass jar with the tip of a paint-brush and place them on their food plant. Put fresh pieces in every day or two, but always plug the neck of the water pot with cotton wool, otherwise the caterpillars may fall in and drown.

Some of the butterflies in Britain hibernate for the winter in the caterpillar stage. If your caterpillars become still and stop eating, simply leave the jar until about March the following year. Then check daily and as soon as the caterpillars start moving again, give them fresh bits of their food plant as before. After a few weeks, they will change into pupae – on a twig, on the lid or side of the jar, or in the soil. Some butterflies hibernate in the pupal stage. When the pupae develop, spray them occasionally with water to stop them drying up and dying. When the adult butterflies emerge, remove the muslin cover so that they can fly away as soon as their wings have expanded and dried.

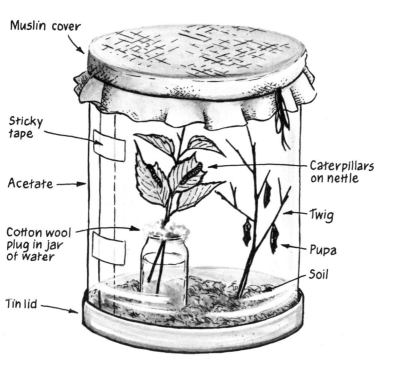

Muslin cover

Sticky tape

Acetate

Cotton wool plug in jar of water

Tin lid

Caterpillars on nettle

Twig

Pupa

Soil

Woodland Quiz

One of these butterflies does not belong in this woodland scene. Do you know which one it is? The answer is upside-down at the bottom of the page.

Purple Emperor

Wood White

Holly Blue

Small Pearl-bordered Fritillary

Speckled Wood

Painted Lady

Painted Lady

54

Name the Butterflies

These butterflies all have very different shapes.
Write each one's name on the line below it. Choose from: Brown Hair-streak, Peacock, Brimstone, Two-tailed Pasha, Comma, Scarce Swallowtail. The answers are upside down at the bottom of the page.

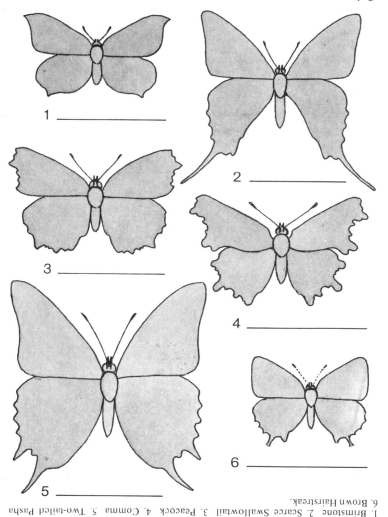

1 _____

2 _____

3 _____

4 _____

5 _____

6 _____

1. Brimstone 2. Scarce Swallowtail 3. Peacock 4. Comma 5. Two-tailed Pasha 6. Brown Hairstreak.

55

Where do Butterflies Lay their Eggs

Match the butterflies with the plants on which they lay their eggs. On the line next to each butterfly, write the letter that belongs to the plant that butterfly prefers. The answers are upside-down at the bottom of the opposite page.

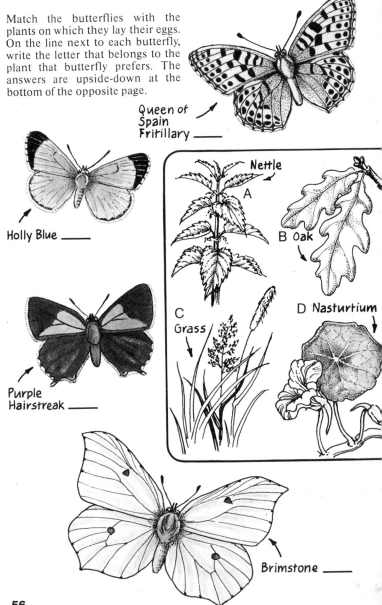

Queen of Spain Fritillary _____

Holly Blue _____

Nettle
A

B Oak

C Grass

D Nasturtium

Purple Hairstreak _____

Brimstone _____

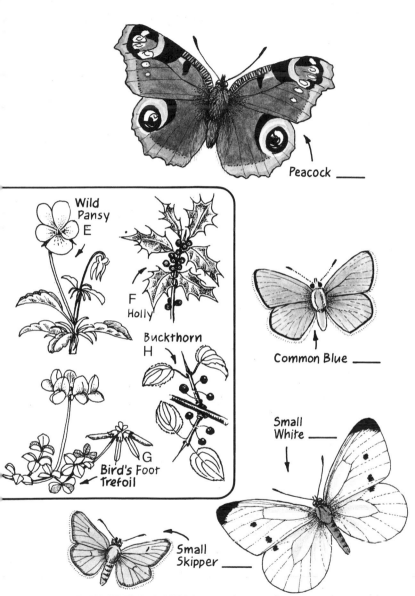

Peacock ____

Wild Pansy
E

F Holly

Buckthorn
H

Bird's Foot
Trefoil
G

Common Blue ____

Small
White ____

Small
Skipper ____

A: Peacock B: Purple Hairstreak C: Small Skipper D: Small White
E: Queen of Spain Fritillary F: Holly Blue G: Common Blue H: Brimstone.

57

Match the Butterflies

The pictures on this page show six butterflies with their wings closed. The same butterflies are shown on the opposite page with their wings open. Can you match them up? Write the number of each butterfly with open wings next to the letter under the correct butterfly with closed wings. The answers are upside-down at the bottom of the opposite page. You could colour the drawing too.

A ____

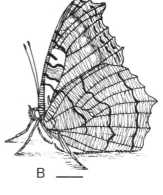

B ____

C ____

D ____

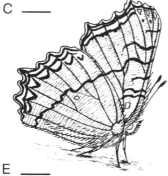

E ____

F ____

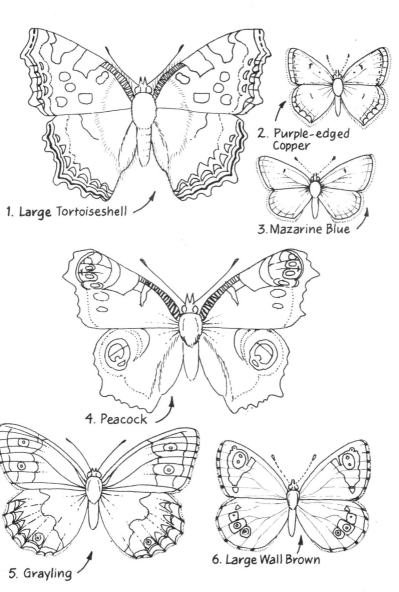

1. **Large** Tortoiseshell

2. Purple-edged Copper

3. Mazarine Blue

4. Peacock

5. Grayling

6. Large Wall Brown

A:5, B:4, C:6, D:2, E:1, F:3.

Glossary

Antenna (plural: antennae) – all butterflies have two antennae on the front of the head, which they use for feeling and smelling.

Camouflage – when the colours and shape of a butterfly, caterpillar or pupa match its background and make it difficult to see.

Colony – a number of butterflies or caterpillars of the same kind living together.

Hibernate – when a butterfly, caterpillar or pupa passes the winter in a sleep-like state.

Larva (plural: larvae) – the larva, or caterpillar, hatches from the butterfly's egg, and the larval stage begins.

Migrant – a butterfly that flies from one country to another, such as the Monarch, which flies from North America to visit Britain.

Migration – the journey of certain butterflies from one country to another. Some butterflies migrate long distances.

Moult – when a caterpillar sheds its skin as it grows larger.

Nectar – a sweet liquid found in most flowers. Butterflies drink it.

Proboscis – a butterfly's long, tube-like tongue, used for sucking nectar.

Pupa (plural: pupae) – the fully-grown larva changes into a pupa, or chrysalis, and the pupal stage begins. The butterfly develops inside the pupa.

Visitor – see **Migrant**

Books to Read

A Field Guide to the Butterflies of Britain and Europe. L. G. Higgins and N. D. Riley (Collins). Very good for identification.
British Butterflies (Books 1 and 2) and *British Caterpillars, Butterflies.* George E. Hyde (Jarrold). Paperbacks with colour photos. Good value.
Butterflies, Moths and their Caterpillars. George E. Hyde (Warne). Small book with photographs and descriptions. Good value.
Butterflies. E. B. Ford (New Naturalist series. Hardback Collins/paperback Fontana). Lots of information about butterflies. For older readers.
The Dictionary of Butterflies and Moths in colour. E. Laithwaite, A. Watson and P. Whalley (Michael Joseph). You could borrow this large book from the library. For older readers.
Looking at Butterflies. Hugh Newman (Collins). British butterflies only.
The NatureTrail Book of Insect Watching. Ruth Thomson (Usborne). How to watch and study insects.
Spotter's Guide to Wild Flowers. Chris Humphries (Usborne).
The Wild Flowers of Britain and Northern Europe. R. and A. Fitter, and M. Blamey (Collins). Both these books are useful for identifying caterpillars' food plants.

Index

Scorecard

The butterflies in this scorecard are arranged in the same order as they appear in the book. When you go spotting, fill in the date at the top of the blank columns, and then write in that column your score, next to each butterfly that you see. At the end of the day, add up your score and put the total at the bottom of the columns. Then add up your grand total.

Page	Butterfly	Score	Date	Date	Date	Page	Butterfly	Score			
5	Monarch	25				14	Silver-washed Fritillary	15			
6	Wall Brown	10				15	Violet Fritillary	25			
6	Large Wall Brown	25				15	Niobe Fritillary	25			
7	Mountain Ringlet	20				15	Cardinal Fritillary	25			
7	Scotch Argus	20				16	Heath Fritillary	25			
8	Speckled Wood	15				16	Marsh Fritillary	20			
8	Arran Brown	20				16	Glanville Fritillary	25			
9	Grayling	15				17	High Brown Fritillary	15			
9	Great Banded Grayling	25				17	Peacock	5			
10	Marbled White	15				18	Painted Lady	15			
10	Large Ringlet	25				18	Red Admiral	10			
11	Meadow Brown	5				18	Small Tortoiseshell	5			
11	Ringlet	10				19	Large Tortoiseshell	25			
11	Small Heath	5				19	Camberwell Beauty	25			
12	Gatekeeper	10				20	Cranberry Fritillary	25			
12	Large Heath	20				20	Lesser Marbled Frit.	25			
13	Queen of Spain Frit.	25				21	Comma	15			
13	Small Pearl-bordered F.	15				21	Lesser Purple Emperor	25			
13	Pearl-bordered Fritillary	15				22	Purple Emperor	25			
14	Dark Green Fritillary	10				22	Duke of Burgundy F.	15			
	Total						Total				

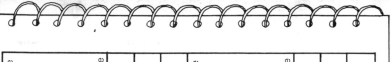

Page	Butterfly	Score				Page	Butterfly	Score			
23	Two-tailed Pasha	25				34	Blue-spot Hairstreak	25			
24	Small Blue	15				35	Swallowtail	25			
24	Idas Blue	25				35	Southern Swallowtail	25			
24	Cranberry Blue	25				36	Scarce Swallowtail	25			
25	Mazarine Blue	25				36	Southern Festoon	25			
25	Amanda's Blue	25				37	Apollo	25			
26	Brown Argus	15				37	Small Apollo	25			
26	Mountain Argus	25				38	Black-veined White	25			
27	Common Blue	5				38	Large White	5			
27	Adonis Blue	20				39	Small White	5			
28	Chalkhill Blue	15				39	Green-veined White	5			
28	Iolas Blue	25				40	Bath White	25			
29	Silver-studded Blue	15				40	Peak White	25			
29	Holly Blue	10				41	Orange Tip	10			
						41	Wood White	20			
30	Scarce Copper	25				42	Pale Clouded Yellow	25			
31	Purple-edged Copper	25				42	Clouded Yellow	20			
31	Small Copper	10				43	Berger's Clouded Y.	25			
32	Green Hairstreak	10				43	Moorland Clouded Y.	25			
32	Brown Hairstreak	20				44	Brimstone	10			
33	Purple Hairstreak	15				44	Cleopatra	25			
33	Black Hairstreak	25				45	Grizzled Skipper	15			
34	White Letter Hairstreak	15				45	Large Grizzled S.	25			
	Total						Total				

Page	Butterfly	Score				Page	Butterfly	Score			
45	Dingy Skipper	10									
46	Chequered Skipper	25									
46	Northern Chequered S.	25									
46	Large Chequered S.	25									
47	Essex Skipper	20									
47	Small Skipper	10									
47	Lulworth Skipper	20									
48	Large Skipper	10									
48	Silver-spotted S.	20									
		Total						Total			
								Grand Total			